Salt-sweat & Tears

Louisa Adjoa Parker

Published by Cinnamon Press
Meirion House
Glan yr afon
Tanygrisiau
Blaenau Ffestiniog
Gwynedd LL41 3SU
www.cinnamonpress.com

The right of Louisa Adjoa Parker to be identified as author of this work has been asserted by her in accordance with the Copyright, Designs and Patent Act, 1988. © 2007, 2016 Louisa Adjoa Parker
ISBN: 978-1-910836-49-1
British Library Cataloguing in Publication Data. A CIP record for this book can be obtained from the British Library

All rights reserved. No part of this publication may be reproduced, stored in a retrieval system, or transmitted in any form or by any means, electronic, mechanical, photocopying, recording or otherwise without either the prior written permission of the publishers. This book may not be lent, hired out, resold or otherwise disposed of by way of trade in any form of binding or cover other than that in which it is published, without the prior consent of the publishers.

Designed & typeset in Palatino by Cinnamon Press. Cover image 'Ripple Rose' © Judy Ben @ Dreamstime.com.

Acknowledgements

I would like to thank Arts Council England for funding the writing of this collection; Jan Fortune for all her invaluable help and support over a number of years; Josie Hickin and the rest of Dorset County Council Arts Team for financial and in-kind support; Selima Hill for her ongoing support over several years; Julia Copus for mentoring me and advising me on my own editing; Joanna Traynor and Steve Martin for their time reading the draft and for their support; Ronnie Goodyer of Reach magazine; Lucy Mackeith and other Black History people in Devon and Exeter for helping me to have confidence in my work; Ruth Katz and the rest of the Lyme Regis poetry group for encouragment with reading; Mark Batey for supporting me; Keziah Bell, Jess Parker and Alicia Parker for putting up with 'Mum and her poetry'; Christina Palfrey for always believing I would write one day; Daniel Parker; my new cousin Kofi Kuranchie and the rest of the family; and finally I would like to thank all the people who are always there, who believe in me and my work: Lottie Prowse, Melissa Merrington-Pink, Clare Johnson, Tarikwa Abebe, Jemima Moore, Sharon Miles, Lisa Faiers, Maisie Hill, Poppy Hanmer and Meika Mills.

Some of the poems have appeared previously in *Coffee House Poetry, Reach, Perhaps* (Cinnamon Press), *Sometimes* (Cinnamon Press), Harmony Newsletter and the 'Small Island read' website.
www.smallislandread.com

Contents

it wasn't to be a bed of pink roses:

English Rose	11
Wedding Dress	12
Trying to be English	13
Memories like muddied stones	14
When he calls me	15
Stroking the cats	16
Just like your father	17
Pieces of reality	18
Falling through ice	19
Teenage Whore	20
Bluebell Woods	21
In our street	22
Jungle	23
Dreaming of skinheads	24
Safe as houses	25

she wants the smell of sea-salt sweat to take the place of her tears:

As I lie waiting	29
On rising from crumpled sheets	30
You said you loved me	31
The smile that never reached his eyes	32
In your pocket	33
Near and far from me	34
Your red mouth	35
Brick Walls	36
Forest-child	37
The Other Woman	38
Cold and blue days	39
Leaving me cold	40

Not seeing me	41
The Little Man's Story	42
Falling silence	44
Under the oak tree	45
Purple Bicycle	46
Fatherless daughters	47
Some people know how it feels	48
Rag Doll	49
Falling Angel	50
Thoughts of a psycho-bitch, early a.m.	51
Boy-angel	52
Chocolate Bath	53
War-torn	54
Skating on Boxing Day	55
Tears at dinner-time	56
Rain-storm	57
Thursday evening	58
People-shaped	59
Family flowering	60

bruising black and white wings against the cage:

Bittersweet	63
In the same breath as it's given, it's taken away	64
If I spin around and jump and shout	65
In the flat-lands	66
Mulatto Girl	67
Velvet Dresses	68
When less is more and more is less	70
Sometimes when I'm making beds	71
On clearing out the garden shed	72
Men like you	73
Pink Roses, in all shades	74

For Keziah, Jessie and Alicia

Salt-sweat & Tears

it wasn't to be a bed of pink roses

English Rose

After he'd married his English Rose
and discovered it wasn't to be
a bed of pink roses,
sometimes he'd blacken
her eyes with bruises like plums
that she would try to hide
under eye-shadow the colour
of bluebottle's wings
and her tortoiseshell specs.

Wedding Dress

When I think of my parents
I think of this:
two people on their wedding day
him, African, proud
with his pink-cheeked English Rose,
her, with brown hair swept sideways,
Sixties style, green eyes flecked with gold.
A white lacy dress clings to her
English pear shape,
lines of piped icing down the sides.
(She will proudly tell us this was a size 10)

When I think of their marriage,
I think of this:
two people seeking entirely
different things
both hell-bent on
Being Right,
each missing every point
the other made.
Juxtaposed like squat battleships
preparing for war,
their Afro'd babies
in the firing line.

Trying to be English

Although he works hard, tries his best
to forget who and what he's left behind,
he can never be the English gentleman
he wants to be;
his brown face forever bobbing
like a buoy in a white, foamy sea;
the English Rose he carries with him
wilting in the cold.

Memories like muddied stones

My memories are like stones in muddied water.
I want to take each one and turn it slowly in my hand,
say *I remember this*:
I remember sitting on a step teaching my sister
to do up the buckles on her fawn Clarks sandals,
clinging like the monkey I thought I was
to my father, telling him
I don't want you to go, when what I meant was
I do, but feel bad for thinking so.

I remember this:
flowered skirts and yellow polo-necks,
brown flared trousers, velvet dresses with lace cuffs,
one red for my sister, blue for me; Seventies' patterned
curtains and walls, I remember neat, short, Afros
for our brother and us, regularly trimmed like hedges,
standing in a corner with my hands raised high above
my head, the brown belt my father used on us,
the smell of Dettol.

I remember this:
the silver poker my father held above my mother's head
while we stood and watched, frozen
into silence, running away from him in darkness, packing
quickly, sitting safely on the Devon-bound train,
I remember the shouting and the bruises like overripe figs,
my father leaving the family home and the weight
of his presence dropping like bricks from our shoulders,
I remember moving without him to the house in Devon,
the red, red earth and sandy beaches a welcome relief,
sliding quickly, like a sock-footed child on a polished floor
                                          into adolescence.

When he calls me

When he calls me,
calls my name so suddenly,
so loudly it makes me fly
around the house, banging into walls
like a bird with wings flapping wildly,
looking for a way out;
I must do what he wants.

When he tells me
to find something
on the cluttered brown island
of a chest of drawers
afloat in the room upstairs,
I must find it straight away
not stand and stare,
and have to pick up each cold object
one by one, I mustn't be
so frightened that I can't see
what I'm looking for.

Stroking the cats

Because I'd stroked the cats
and not washed my hands,
he wiped each silver door-handle
with brown Dettol
that smelt of hospital wards,
then hit my hand with a plastic ruler,
so that I'd learn to be nice
and clean, like him.

Just like your father

How could we—
three brown children
with afros,
like black woolly sheep,
(or so they said)
sitting on our heads,
Seventies coconut-kids,
with soft shells that didn't need
to be hit with a hammer to break
—how could we grow up
not thinking *black* equals *bad*
when she would tell us
we were just like him?

*You're just like your black
bastard of a Dad*, she'd say.

Pieces of reality

She snaps at us this morning,
grinding her teeth
like a dog waiting to bite.
Spittle foams around her lips
like bubbles in silt-mud.

She looks at us, hisses,
spits out the words
I wish you'd Never Been Born.
They fall, clattering, to the floor
and shatter into jagged pieces;

I pick them up and press them to my skin.

Falling through ice

Whilst trying to *get us*
and wanting somehow to hurt us,
she fell through the glass door
like a hippo falling through ice
in a half-frozen lake,
finding herself wishing
that the water wasn't so cold.

Teenage Whore

Because I was trying to Become A Woman,
painted my eyes like a panda bear,
smoked cigarettes and drank apple-cider
until I was sick; loved too many men:

because I was becoming someone
you didn't want me to become,
you'd break my things,
call me a whore.

Bluebell Woods

Amongst damp brown leaves
in bluebell woods
we played and scratched and fought,
we learned of our desire—
muddy hands fluttered like moths
inside our clothes;
heat-seeking-lust-seeking-skin
                on skin.

Oh, the games we played that year
us girls and boys;
you had no idea.

In our street

The kids in our street would call us
a whole dung-heap of names—
Nigger, Blackie, Wog and *Coon*
were the favourites, nestled amongst the rest,
brought out from time to time
and brandished bravely
like a child's plastic sword
to protect them from our blackness.

There were jokes galore about the time
being *half-caste-two*,
and they'd ask if the browness
washed off in the bath;
but the kids in our street still played
with us *blackies,*
with our hair like frightened sheep,
who were just beginning to learn
it was impolite to have been born;
and they still came to our house for tea.

Jungle

I'd feel confused when they'd tell me
to go back to the jungle
and make monkey noises.
Where I came from the only jungle
was made of concrete and coal dust
and grey smoky air,
and there weren't any monkeys
in South Yorkshire
that *I* knew of.

Dreaming of skinheads

At night, I'd dream of being chased
by gangs of skinhead men,
and my Afro, like a soft foam ball,
would seem bigger in the darkness
as the stamp of their
Doc-Martened feet
came closer.

Safe as houses

We took holidays at our Grandparents
in Devon; the bungalow was clean as a pin—
dust didn't dare settle for long.
We'd wake to the smell of bacon
(for vegetarians this wasn't meant
to be a Good Thing,
but the smell of frying pigs
comforted us nevertheless.)
We'd eat toast and marmalade
with real butter, thick as a book,
drink tea from bone-china cups,
lock each other in a pantry lined
with treats, like a house made of gingerbread
we picked sweet foods from its walls.

Safer than my childhood homes,
safer than any houses, this white house in Devon
with its garden roses, circled with red earth.
At the back an apple orchard lined our path
to see the trains.

I can see them now, Phyllis and Bert,
waving from the doorstep;
getting smaller as we drove away,
like a wedding cake couple, white-haired,
smiling, on their red-brick steps.

she wants the smell of sea-salt
sweat to take the place of her tears:

As I lie waiting

As you reach
into the drawer, fumbling,
all I can see
as I lie here waiting
in this white desert of a bed,
are your buttocks
beneath your T-shirt
like two white pear-halves
floating in sugar-syrup.

On rising from crumpled sheets

She offers herself to him shyly,
eyes cast downwards
like a handmaid holding out a sweet
on a white china plate,
(who virtually asked
for it to be snatched up,
eaten greedily with much
smacking of lips, and spittle flying.)
She lies, afterwards, umoving,
unmoved, on crumpled white sheets.
She looks at him, sleeping
beside her with his parted lips
like fat slugs
that trailed their way around her,
his fingers like sharp sticks
that pressed her skin,
trying to make her his.

I'm not yours she thinks,
rising from the crumpled sheets.

You said you loved me

Because
you said you loved me
in the graveyard that day
while you clutched a cider bottle
as though it were gold
with your hair falling down
your back like brown water,

because
I needed to hear that
I fell into your life
like a stone sinking in a river.

The smile that never reached his eyes

You smiled
at me that night, smelling
of whisky and salt-sweat,
that was all it took—
a glance from your cold blue eyes
like those of a fish lying on crushed ice,
and I glided cleanly into your life
like a hot knife through butter.
And yes, you beat me, your
fists banging on my head
like pebbles on glass,
and yes,
you drank, brown rivers of whisky
on which hate-smeared words floated
like old prams in a canal.
And yes, yes
there were women.

But I stayed
even when the smile
(which never quite reached
your fish-blue eyes)
had long gone,
because I strangely believed
you loved me.

In your pocket

like an old boiled sweet
coated in hairs and dust
you take me out of your pocket
from time to time
and suck me for a while.

Near and far from me

How can you sleep every night
in my bed, your skin brushing mine,
like two orchids curling in the heat
(dreaming of separate lives)?
How can you be sleeping so close to me
yet be this far away,
while I lie next to you, stranded,
like a flat fish struggling to breathe
flapping its tail on wet sand?

Your red mouth

You watch me
with narrow eyes
like a cat
about to pounce,
and I know, any minute
you'll pick me up
in your red, wet, mouth
drag me to a quiet corner
and rip out my insides.

Brick Walls

When I see you,
my face is oil-slicked with make-up
the colours of an Eighties' dream
(I have to look eighteen)
All the men stare,
the sight of a woman is a treat
when you're locked away
you say.

When I see you
you're wearing a toothpaste-striped shirt—
I have never seen you looking so clean.
Babies in pushchairs
with pink plastic dummies cry;
we stare at pale-green brick walls
trying hard to think
of what not to say,
eat kit-kats
and everybody smokes.

Forest-child

That night we made you
in the forest,
lying in the orange two-man tent
in the middle of tall trees
dark like patterned cloth.

I woke next morning
listening to woodpigeons
rolling the sounds of summer
like toffees in their throats.
(The first time I ever really heard
the rhythm of their coos.)

      I dreamed you into being—
a child-shaped star falling
through the forest sky, lighting it with hope
like a Catherine wheel;
finding me, finding your home in me.

The Other Woman

i
Molehills

    that night before you tell
me about her you smash up my
mother's house, rip bookshelves from
the walls, kick and scream as though you
can smash and scream your guilt into oblivion,
while i stand here (frightened and not frightened)
hoping against hope that you won't rip the baby from me.
you phone her then to come and get you from my mother's
house while pain drips from me like scalding water
i pick up the books the piles of books
like molehills on the sitting room floor.

ii
Her Red Curls

i crumple
as you wave from the back seat
of the blue car you climbed into with her,
try to fold the pain in half, myself
in half, i sink to the pavement crying and
clutching my belly the fat warmness of our child
trying to keep her away from the pain.
you are still waving, smiling, while the memory
of her red curls singes me like hot iron.

Cold and blue days

On days like these
she just wants to lie
on a bed of tiny stones,
under a cold, blue waterfall
and cry, and let the coldness
wash her tears away.

On days like these
she just wants to dive
into a half-frozen lake,
and swim under the ice
amongst green weeds like fingers
that stroke her legs, and cry,
and let the coldness
freeze her pain.

Leaving me cold

You spent a good half an hour
rummaging and foraging around down there,
while I lay, unmoved
like a cold wet spotted fish,
eyes glazed over, unmoving on a plate.

I wanted to wriggle and squirm,
flap my tail wetly
and gasp for breath.
I wouldn't say I was thinking of England,
but I certainly wasn't thinking of you.

Not seeing me

With your eyes firmly focused
on the pavement beneath your feet,
you walk past me,
not seeing, or pretending
you can't see
that I'm carrying your child.

The Little Man's Story

You left a trail of lemon-bitter
women behind you, scattered
like beer bottles all over town,
sharp-edged, rattling in the wind.
You didn't quite manage to smash
them into little pieces, although,
God knows, you tried.

They bore your children, some of them.
You charmed them, snake-like,
waited until they felt safe, then moved
in to fill them with poison, preying
on the insecure, the needy, the slightly
fucked up.

You had Little Man Syndrome:
a cocky strut and an arrogance
that was bigger than you were;
like a handed-down coat
several sizes too big, you swam
around in it, flapping its sleeves.

Your need, your desire to control them—
was it part of a Plan To Take
Over The World, starting with your
current bird, by clipping her wings?
Or was a bid to get the attention
your father never gave you as a child?
History repeating itself, his story
your story;
boasting about the size of your prick
as though it would compensate
for your lack of height,
lack of heart.

Falling silence

With his face set
like the blue-lias stone
his heart is made of,
he walks past his child;
her face lights up like a yellow daffodil
bursting into bloom
then withering to brown,
as his silence falls on her
and eats into her
like acid rain.

Under the oak tree

the day i went to your funeral i met your life,
it flashed before me, danced and paraded
winking before me, it was a carnival
of colours and faces, cigarettes and sad smiles:
a multitude of friends with bright coloured
dreadlocks piled high on their heads
like proud snakes;
and me, as if behind a thick glass wall,
watching the parade with blurry eyes.

the day i went to your funeral i met your parents,
your dad all grey with cigarettes and tears,
your mum round, with raven-black hair,
stretching smiles to hide their pain.
your life as a jigsaw with one missing piece;
and me, all breasts and belly
swollen with our child, salt tears
like warm sea water trickling down my face,
under a giant oak tree in the quiet cemetery,
watching your life without you in it.

Purple Bicycle

I dream
after his death,
of riding a purple bicycle
along a river path
and shouting his name
so loudly it fills the sky
like red smoke from an aeroplane,
in the hope that he might hear.

Fatherless daughters

Without knowing I was doing it I strove
to make my children fatherless
like me; was the absence of theirs
so different from the absence I felt as a child?
You were alive, breathing, filling the house
with frustration like the smoke
from burning stubble in the fields around our house.

You were always just out of reach,
your heavy presence used as a threat:
a means of being un-loved;
you folded yourself away from us
like just-ironed clothes.

Dad—a word I struggled to use—
now fills my children's mouths
like the acrid smell of burning fields.

Some people know how it feels

to bear children alone,
to be a child-parent,
to watch your daughters cry
for their fathers, each loving theirs
in their separate ways;
to flap nervously
like a trapped bird
in the face of all this father-less-ness.

Some people know how it feels
to hate the man, or men, who went,
to want to drive silver-tipped stakes
through their hearts for doing so,
kill them all over again
for leaving little girls behind
without their Daddies;
to want to take the living one, slam
him against a red-brick wall
extract love painfully from him like tree sap;
to keep all the pain wrapped up tight,
like a rosebud.

Some people know how it feels
to be a single mother.

Rag Doll

How they throw her to one another
these men she goes to,
and laugh as she soars between them
like a rag doll,
all long cotton arms and
woolly braids trying their best
to stream gracefully in the air.

As she lands at their feet
they prod life into her, these men.
When they call her a beauty she smiles,
her painted dolly-pink mouth not quite reaching
her black spider-lashed eyes.

She tries to suck
drops of love from them, this doll-girl,
like a baby sucks milk,
tries to fill the hole in her cotton-wool heart,
wants the smell of sea-salt sweat
to take the place of her tears.

How prettily she flits between them
this woman-doll, a butterfly basking
in a sun of admiration
though she wakes each lonely morning,
with all her stuffing gone.

Falling Angel
for Si

i hope the angels caught you
when you jumped
i hope they surrounded you
in a glittering cloud,
all white fluffy wings and
fat-cheeked smiles

as you made your way
past rows and rows of cars
quietly glinting in the dark
like foil-wrapped sweets

i hope they laid you gently down
when you landed
your cheek resting on the tarmac
as though a feather bed
i hope they stroked your face
and soothed you
when you spoke those last words
to those who found you—

I'm not in any pain.

Thoughts of a psycho-bitch, early a.m.

As I lie waiting for you to come home
after spending the night with the darkness
pressing close to my face
like a black crushed-velvet dress
smelling of must, a list
of Things I Want to do to Hurt You
writes itself, unbidden, in my head:
I want to (1) cut the head off the cream
teddy bear you gave me last Valentine's,
break apart the bunch of roses it holds
between its paws; (2) pack your clothes
and collection of trainers into black plastic bags,
stuff them so full they split, leaking clothes
like secrets onto the pavement outside;
(3) bolt all the doors (only I have no bolts,
so I'll have to bolt my mind instead);
(4) carry your heart—the heart that was meant
to beat with love for me, the heart
that always put me first—
in one of my shoes and walk for miles,
each step crushing it as you have crushed mine,
until it is like raspberry jelly, pink,
cool and gelatinous between my toes.

Boy-angel

I used to think you just stopped short
of being a miracle, a Divine Being,

a boy-angel sent to me, in clean socks and a shy
smile— not only did I put you on a pedestal, I paraded

you through towns, cities, in hand-drawn carriages,
dressed you in robes and jewels, I crowned

you, celebrated your existence, wanted you
to carry me with you;

                now, you have fallen
from the carriage, grazed your Divine knees,

the robes have turned to limp grey rags, the jewels
were nothing more than costume jewellery—I realise

it is I who has to carry you, carry your emotions, your
fucked-up-ness as well as mine, in my heart.

Chocolate Bath

I will not allow myself
to luxuriate in sadness again,
like a chocolate bath
coating me—
a second, darker, skin—
I will not allow myself the luxury,
the bittersweet cocoa of pain.

War-torn

While everything around me crumbles,
I will stand like a lone building
in a war-torn landscape
—a land where the people are so tired
of the bombs and the landmines
and the rat-tat-tatting of machine guns
blasting them from life, so tired
of seeing smooth-cheeked boys
with guns strapped with insouciance
to their chests, tired of the mothers holding
shrouded children like shop-wrapped gifts,
rocking (as though they can rock their way
into another existence.) I will give
myself a weekly ration of tears then,
like a survivor of war, I will get up,
wash the blood from my skin, the mud-streaked tears
from my face, forage for food in the red dust.
I will do what each of us can choose to do—survive,
in a landscape striped with the colours of pain.

Skating on Boxing Day

We should have known
we couldn't spend two, whole, fat days
boxed inside tinsel-lined walls
like greetings cards pressed flat
on top of each other,
smiling and nodding and passing
the cranberry sauce;

skating around issues
of our family's past
like skaters
on just-frozen ice.

Tears at dinner-time

At dinner
my brother looks at my father,
tears clotting in his throat like drying glue,
and becomes his boy-self, asking his Daddy
why he'd left him
to bring up the family he'd discarded
like old clothes.
My brother, a tall, proud man
with long dreadlocks like liquorice snakes
uncoiling from his head
cries a hot fistful of tears.

At dinner
my father looks at my brother,
pirouettes his food around his plate,
until he's had *enough of this*.
My father
doesn't comfort this boy-man, his boy,
his only living son,
but instead flies into a rage
that fizzes around the dinner table
like angry bees.

Rain-storm

When he shouted
at dinner, my little girl-self
couldn't hold back any longer,
she was so scared of this Daddy-monster,
(whom she thought existed
only in her memories, her dreams;
she hadn't invited this monster to dinner)
that she burst into a rain-storm
of hot clouded tears,
that poured down her face
and into the food,
so neatly arranged
on her blue-flowered china plate.

Thursday evening

     and during the phone call
with my father
(rare, with him)
he drops the bombshell casually,
as someone else might drop
litter in the street—
without knowing,
(or caring)
where it lands:

Your brother's in Ghana,
he's found your Aunt

—as though it were my aunt
and our entire family,
not him,
who had mislaid themselves
for over thirty years.

People-shaped

All of a sudden the people-shaped spaces
in my head are filled with life;
like chalked outlines on the ground
they get up, fill out, unfold;
steam-rollered animations
popping back into shape.

This life-giving knowledge—
it's the opposite of death.

Family flowering

I've never had an aunt before,
nor cousins nor uncles
nor cousins-once-removed;
now I have so many they fill my head
like flowers bursting into bloom;
I want to pick them one
by one, learn them off by heart
then press them with care
between scraps of tissue paper,
like fine white lace;
preserve them in the folds of my life.

bruising black and white wings
against the cage:

Bittersweet

How can the words
my and *sister*
roll so easily on his tongue
like honeyed sweets?

He didn't tell his children much —
the name of an African capital here
an aunt or uncle there—
less than a fistful of knowledge
for us to keep,
dust-coated and strange,
close to our hearts.

Now they've been returned to him
he picks them up with casual thanks,
like brown-papered parcels lost in the post
for over thirty years;

I try them for myself;
the unfamiliar names
that roll so easily on his tongue
leave a bitter aftertaste
on mine.

In the same breath as it's given, it's taken away

It's like
being handed a gold-wrapped
gift, tied with curling white ribbons and encrusted
with jewels, knowing everything you didn't
know you always wanted, was inside,
then having it snatched back,
the paper ripped, the gift
thrown to the ground, watching
as it's stamped on, crushed by heavy-booted feet—
hearing you had another sister
and now she is dead.

If I spin around and jump and shout
for Rosina

if i spin around quickly
enough will i catch sight of you,
my ghost-sister, smiling behind me
before you fade like cotton in the sun?
if i jump, keep on jumping,
until my head just peeps
over the top of this world, will i
find myself staring into brown eyes
like mine? if i close my eyes and train
my ears to pick out minuscule pieces
of forgotten sound from the past,
like splinters of glass, will I hear you
cry? if i shout your name, keep on shouting,
will you hear, will you know
                of my sorrow?

In the flat-lands

While we were busy being frightened
in the flat-lands of East Anglia
with its burning fields and willowy trees
weeping their leaves like tears into rivers;
its white criss-cross bridges and the Stranger
down at the Rec,
with oranges in his pockets
that we had to, at all costs, ignore—

while we were busy being frightened
by someone much closer to home:
your father, yours and ours,
who'd left you in his homeland
to try and grow,
who believed you'd be fine without him
fine without a father, or a mother;

you were less than sixty miles away
from the flat-lands, where the fields burned
all around us when summers went,
hopelessly searching for the man
you'd never find;
the man we'd run upstairs to hide from
every day, when he came home.

Mulatto Girl

See the mulatto girl walking
down country lanes and fields, her
head held high, her skin the colour
of caramel boiling on the stove. See her smile
in the knowledge she is not the first
to walk this green and pleasant
countryside, she has history stirring within her limbs.
she has Africa's heat and England's cold rain
pumping through her blood, her
DNA a beautiful mix of gene pools
scattered across continents. She is strong.
She shows Africa in a way the English hide.
She shows an eighteenth century master's love for slaves.
She shows a slave's contempt.
She shows twentieth century people brave enough
to cross a line made of different tones of skin,
to love in spite of hate.

See the mulatto girl walking
down country lanes and fields, her head
held high, her quadroon baby girls
held on her hips, her hair thick and frizzed, lips
half full, there are no
white men dressing her in robes and jewels,
but see her smile, see her sway, as she walks
with her head held high.

Velvet Dresses

I want to climb under Dorset's skin
curl up in her folds, wrap her around me
like a patchwork quilt, stained
yet stitched with years of love,
taste the colours of green and gold,
run my fingers over rough textures
of ancient earth.

I want to crawl under her pavements,
her roads; lift great slabs of Tarmac,
climb every craggy, awkward hill,
every cliff like a tooth capped with gold;
trek for miles through woods
and green fields like velvet dresses
with skirts fanned out wide;

I want to sink my fingers into the earth,
let the tiny stones and grit and bones
run through my hands;
search for the past along with
fossils spiralling to dust
in clay-rich soil.

I want to let Dorset's past soak
like cocoa butter into my skin,
let its history merge with mine:
talk of Africa and her slaves.

I want to know it will be fine
for anyone with *not from here* etched
like tribal markings into their skin,
to sink into Dorset like a warm rock-pool,
with fingers stretched out towards the sun;
to walk her beaches, green-velvet fields
with pride, say,

I live here, I belong here, she is mine.

When less is more and more is less

In this part of the world, some women
wear their thinness with pride,
like designer clothes, their bones
jutting awkwardly like tent poles in carrier bags;
they are sharp-edged, brittle,
we admire them for their neat waists, their conservative
approach to food, their ability to starve slowly
in a country filled with food— we are sickened
                              yet enthralled
by their boy-hips, full lips in tiny faces,
in awe of these creatures.
They are hollow, like straws; thin-faced cherubs;

by taking up less space they somehow seem bigger.

Then there are women the size of buses, their
upper arms great slabs of meat, stomachs
unrolling like hills over elasticated waists.
They move slowly, in groups, pack-like;
we whisper they should join a slimming club,
                          envy them cake,
watch reality TV and see pounds falling from strangers,
weigh ourselves, pinch inches, count fat grams,
try to decide whether or not to eat.
While the rest of the world watches, choice-less,
and starves.

Sometimes when I'm making beds

    or pressing hot creases into sheets
like a young girl's secrets wrapped in paper,
while the smell of heated cotton warms the room;
sometimes I think, were it not for the sounds
of cars outside, and the television sets
like squat black beetles in each of the rooms,
the vacuum cleaner I drag behind me
like a reluctant dog being walked; were it not for these—
I could be an African servant girl
brought back two centuries ago
from Jamaican plantations by a trader,
my master, his mulatto child in fact.
The view over Lyme Bay, misty now,
is much the same as it must have been then,
the neatly trimmed hedges and lawns,
lavender beds and the red-earthed driveway
curling around flowerbeds like a slowworm, sleepy
in the heat; the rooms with their polished dressers,
curved legs and white lace mats, the sounds of birds,
the clock in the hall.
Little has changed here, up at the big house
with me, the servant girl, being treated jolly well,
having praise heaped on me, like spoonfuls of sugar,
for washing clothes, or folding sheets well,
while I make beds and think I know
how the magpie they keep in the garden
wrapped in wire must feel,
bruising its black and white wings against the cage,
pretending I was born for this;
smiling and dusting and cleaning white people's rooms,
with the smell of hot cotton warming my skin,
pressing hot creases like frown lines into sheets.

On clearing out the garden shed

I'm sweeping and sorting the past into piles.
A white plastic bag full of baby clothes
sits accusingly in the corner,
in the half-dark of the shed.
The clothes are so rotted some are
unrecognisable: some are fine grey tatters
like spider webs, others spongy, greased
with white mould. Furred toys with glaring
plastic eyes lie dotted around
like the corpses of rodents.
The cobwebs are so thick they catch on nails
when I brush them, suspended on walls
like smoky-grey stockings thrown from a bed.
Oh, but the yellow brushed-cotton sheet
with blue rabbits, I can allow myself that,
the memory of my eldest daughter sleeping
that catches in my throat like a scream,
though I carry on clearing, I tell myself
that what's past is past, that the little girl
who left her purse stuffed with coppers
and a single, creased dollar in the corner
of this shed not so long ago has been replaced
by a soon-to-be adult.
A small glimmer of hope
that she'll be fine, grow strong without me,
glints like the piece of glass
on the shed floor, catching the sun.

Men like you

everywhere i go you're there,
a black-haired, starling-faced
suitably sad-eyed
great hulk of a reminder
that i didn't do enough
to protect my daughter
(and other people's daughters)
from men like you.

Pink Roses, in all shades

Just because
there are roses growing

up the red-brick wall in the garden,
on a sun-blasted trellis blown over

by the wind, in all shades of the warmest
of pinks—from almost white to a deep

sun-rose—it doesn't mean I have to stay
for the roses; people are born, people grow,

people die. They move house, move in and out
of each other's lives

like little fish darting among weeds, we
move on. Roses grow. Sometimes there is more

to be gained than lost by leaving. Roses
can grow anywhere.

www.ingramcontent.com/pod-product-compliance
Ingram Content Group UK Ltd.
Pitfield, Milton Keynes, MK11 3LW, UK
UKHW021325180426
11947UKWH00017B/1447